CALEB LEWIS is a multi-award-winning writer whose plays have been produced locally and internationally. Mentored by Nick Enright and Edward Albee, Lewis is a former resident playwright at Griffin Theatre and the 2015 writer in residence at Red Stitch Actors Theatre. He has twice been shortlisted for the Griffin Award and is the winner of an Inscription Award, the Mitch Mathews Award, an Ink Award and an AWGIE (Australian Writers' Guild Award). He is the inaugural winner of the Richard Burton Award for New Plays. His plays include *Nailed*, *Dogfall*, *Death in Bowengabbie*, *Songs for the Deaf*, *Aleksander and the Robot Maid*, *Destroyer of Worlds*, *Clinchfield* and *Rust and Bone*.

Kris McQuade as Maggie Stone and Mark Saturno as Leo Hermes in State Theatre Company of South Australia's 2013 production at the Space Theatre, Adelaide. (Photo: Matt Nettheim)

MAGGIE STONE

Caleb Lewis

CURRENCY PLAYS

First published in 2015
by Currency Press Pty Ltd,
PO Box 2287, Strawberry Hills, NSW, 2012, Australia
enquiries@currency.com.au
www.currency.com.au

Copyright: Introduction © Murray Bramwell, 2015; *Maggie Stone* © Caleb Lewis, 2013, 2015.

COPYING FOR EDUCATIONAL PURPOSES

The Australian *Copyright Act 1968* (Act) allows a maximum of one chapter or 10% of this book, whichever is the greater, to be copied by any educational institution for its educational purposes provided that that educational institution (or the body that administers it) has given a remuneration notice to Copyright Agency Limited (CAL) under the Act.
For details of the CAL licence for educational institutions contact CAL, Level 15/233 Castlereagh Street, Sydney, NSW, 2000; tel: within Australia 1800 066 844 toll free; outside Australia 61 2 9394 7600; fax: 61 2 9394 7601; email: info@copyright.com.au

COPYING FOR OTHER PURPOSES

Except as permitted under the Act, for example a fair dealing for the purposes of study, research, criticism or review, no part of this book may be reproduced, stored in a retrieval system, or transmitted in any form or by any means without prior written permission. All enquiries should be made to the publisher at the address above.

Any performance or public reading of *Maggie Stone* is forbidden unless a licence has been received from the author or the author's agent. The purchase of this book in no way gives the purchaser the right to perform the play in public, whether by means of a staged production or a reading. All applications for public performance should be addressed to Keightley Management, 139 Cathedral Street, Woolloomooloo NSW 2011, Australia; ph: 61 2 8302 2800; email: mkm@mollison.com.au

Cataloguing-in-publication data for this title is available from the National Library of Australia website: www.nla.gov.au

Typeset by Dean Nottle for Currency Press.
Cover photo: Kris Washusen.
Cover shows Kris McQuade as Maggie Stone.
Cover design by Miranda Costa.

Currency Press acknowledges the Traditional Owners of the Country on which we live and work. We pay our respects to all Aboriginal and Torres Strait Islander Elders, past and present.

Contents

Introduction
  Murray Bramwell   vii

Writer's Notes
  Caleb Lewis   xiii

MAGGIE STONE

Act One: A Loan   1
Act Two: Black   14
Act Three: The Deficiency   41
Act Four: Red   54

Kris McQuade as Maggie Stone and Shedrick Yarkpai as Benny in State Theatre Company of South Australia's 2013 production at the Space Theatre, Adelaide. (Photo: Matt Nettheim)

The Rising Debt of Gratitude: Actions and Transactions in *Maggie Stone*

It was Polonius in *Hamlet* who said, 'Neither a borrower nor a lender be;/ For loan oft loses both itself and friend'. He is right, of course, but, like much of the old man's advice to the young prince, it is a platitude, something easier said than done. It is not how we live in the world because the world won't let us.

In his insightful, engaging, sometimes grimly humorous play *Maggie Stone*, Caleb Lewis tells us a story of present-day Australia that is rarely heard despite the refugee experience woven into Australian history, particularly the last seventy-five years. This country has seen waves of resettlement since the Second World War—large numbers of Greek and Italian immigrants and, in the early 1970s, Vietnamese—but this is rarely acknowledged as the truly nation-building achievement that it is.

Each of these historic phases of population growth has brought immense benefits to Australia's culture and economy, but they have also been met with resentment, ignorance and fear. Indeed, the 'White Australia' policy was only finally rescinded by the Whitlam Government in 1973.

In the 21st century Australia is more multicultural than ever, with migration continuing not only from the UK and Europe, but China, South-East Asia, the Middle East and South Saharan Africa. Yet still, particularly over the last fifteen years, social and political tensions persist. Border protection, stopping refugee boats and accusations of links with terrorism are daily headlines even as I write this introduction.

Maggie Stone is a timely play that speaks to the xenophobia and resistance that all communities experience when they are confronted with people and cultures that are unfamiliar and often, unfairly, deemed hostile to prevailing values, beliefs and customs.

In the character of Maggie Stone, Caleb Lewis has brought together an array of Anglo-Saxon Australian traits. She is staunchly loyal, no-nonsense, practical and ready to take action; she is also bigoted, suspicious and instinctively negative.

So when, in the opening scene of the play, she meets the Sudanese refugee Prosper Deng in her office at the bank, she makes the immediate assumption that he is a cleaner, there to empty the bins. Presented with his desperate request for a loan to fix his car so he can get to work, and exasperated by the complexity of his problems, she promptly refuses him.

The ensuing chain of events leading to Prosper's death and the subsequent efforts by his widow—the determined, resourceful Amath—to support herself and her teenage son Benny, give human faces and emotions to the spiralling nightmare we call the poverty cycle; the cruel logic that, once you get into debt, it is more likely to escalate than ever be reversed.

Several experiences prompted Lewis to create this play. The first was when he was an intern working alongside a woman who was in charge of debt collection for the firm. As he recalls,

> She had a different title, but that's what she did—she made the hard calls. I was fascinated by her. She was sharp and fierce and she didn't suffer fools, but at the same time she had this incredible capacity for loyalty. I had a lot of lunch conversations with her about various organisations she had worked for, some of which were pretty tough. And I became interested in the whole world of debt collection and debt and poverty.*

So he had found the benevolent side of Maggie, to which he added the more tangled attributes and conflicts that the character experiences because of her own emotional and financial debts and obligations. Similarly, the character of Amath Deng grew from his work as a volunteer at the Sudanese Australian Integrated Learning Centre (SAIL) in Blacktown, Sydney. His task was to help migrants, almost always women, with conversational English. Reflecting on that time he says,

> I had gone in naïvely and, if I'm honest with myself, somewhat opportunistically, thinking, 'Great, I will be able to ask these people about their lives and get the stuff for my play'. And what I quickly realised was that these women had far more pressing concerns than talking about the past. They needed to know how to pay bills, how to get jobs, what this note or report said that

---

* Personal interview, May 7, 2015. All subsequent quotes from this conversation.

had been sent home from school about their kids. These pressing needs were on them straightaway and I was caught out. I realised I wanted something from them too. There's a line in the play when Amath says, 'Back in Kenya—in the camps—they say we can stay there for free. But everybody wants something. The journalists want our stories; the NGOs want us to sing in their choirs; the SPLA wants our sons as soldiers. The spirits of our ancestors want us to honour them…' I realised I also had come in looking for a relationship that was transactional in nature. I had to forget about that and just talk English!

But Lewis also gained insight into the abruptness of the immigration process:

People in camps would be invited into a portable office, watch a documentary about Australia for about two hours, and then be flown there. Someone picked them up at the airport and took them to their house. Suddenly they are in this whole new world and in many ways left to fend on their own. So if you don't have church or mosque or strong cultural ties, in many ways you are marooned.

In the play it is Amath who exhibits the resilience and inner strength to adapt under difficult circumstances. Like so many of the women Lewis met at SAIL she quickly learns the social skills needed, taking up responsibilities traditionally seen as matters for men only. She is in marked contrast to Maggie, who is outwardly strong but privately anxious and vulnerable. Skilfully, and using a mix of humour, pathos and suspense, Lewis makes the interaction and increasing trust between the two women the heart of the story.

As Lewis observes, Maggie is the character he uses to guide the audience into the unfamiliar world of Amath and her family. Tetchy, stubborn, rude, casually racist, she is, nonetheless, the devil we know.

I didn't want to write with a central protagonist who was from somewhere else, I wasn't prescient about that world and, to be honest, the predominantly white audience who will be attending would want a touchstone, someone they can identify with and who can take them through the story.

Initially Maggie's contact with the Deng family is routine however, when confronted with the tragic ripple effect of her loan refusal, she has deep misgivings. Her motives for involvement begin with a sense of guilt but ultimately her commitment to Amath and Benny is a discovery of her better self. Only gradually are we made aware of Maggie's own previous entanglement with the loan shark Leo Hermes, a toxic obligation formed in order to pay for the continuing care of her paralysed brother. Just like Prosper's desperate robbery, she is duty-bound to help her family, even if it means doing crazy things with dreadful consequences. Lewis comments on her abiding insecurities and suspicions:

> Beneath the surface there is this desperate feeling of owing others, of being in a situation where she is powerless, not in control, so the only way she can maintain that power is to isolate herself. I read a great essay by Michael Flood called *Mapping Loneliness in Australia*. It shows that, despite the fact that cities are getting busier and there are more people, we are becoming more isolated than ever. Rather than being a great continent of people, we have become a kind of urban archipelago with thousands of isolated islands.

A central theme in *Maggie Stone* is the vexed question of charity itself. 'It is a complicated business,' says Lewis,

> … and I use the word 'business' consciously. I was interested in the idea of 'charity wounds'—what you do to a person, or a people, and how the relationship changes between the giver and recipient. When you accept the help of others it puts you in a vulnerable position, one that can be easily exploited. Maggie exploits that position by trying to get Amath to sign the letter. Georgina exploits it by dominating Amath—Maggie refers to 'your little rent-a-friend'.

Georgina's place in this web of reciprocation is particularly interesting. She is well-meaning—as she herself insists:

> Let me tell you—I'm a good person. I am. I give to UNICEF. I donate to Greenpeace, I buy dolphin-safe tuna and free-range eggs—even though they're more expensive. And pink ribbons for breast cancer, red ribbons for AIDS and the white one for—I forget what it's for but I always pin one on!

But as Caleb Lewis notes, from the audience feedback from the Adelaide performances, she was the character most distrusted and disliked.

> That took me by surprise. Georgina is like a lot of people in any city in Australia. There is a lot of her in me. We have good intentions but not a lot of interest or engagement in the back stories and where they fit in. Georgina wants Amath to fit into a back story she has already written for her.

Perhaps the reaction to Georgina is a measure of our frustration, if not despair, over our ability to contribute usefully in catastrophic situations or, to use that hackneyed phrase, 'to make a difference'. It is easy enough to lampoon Georgina as a 'do-gooder'—a curiously derogatory term in the Australian context—but are we all now just do-nothings? It was former army chief David Morrison who recently said, 'The standard you walk past is the standard you accept'. And it is a telling remark.

But the dilemma for providers of charity and foreign aid is always how to make it useful to the recipients. A good start is to ask them directly what they need and to understand better how the assistance fits the given circumstances. The story of the mosquito nets, which Amath tells, is almost like a parable of unintended consequences. Lewis notes, 'There is a predisposition to throw money at problems and hope they go away, when we need a more sustained face-to-face engagement'.

In Act One of *Maggie Stone* the narrative seems to be on a particularly dismal trajectory. But Lewis is not bound by naturalistic determinism. As a playwright he has an impish talent for keeping us engaged, even when the prospects are awful. His comedy and whimsicality, far from neutralising or negating the serious issues he raises, leaven them and reframe the possibilities. We need only look at the character names to see this is not strict realism—'Maggie Stone' with her cold-hearted surname, 'Leo Hermes' may have the name of a Greek messenger of the gods but he sounds like a flashy expensive wristwatch and the time is running out, 'Prosper Deng' is sardonically misnamed ('Deng' we are told means 'rain') and 'Georgina Spack' is in there papering over the cracks.

Maggie Stone's unexpected ending—a wish-fulfilment resolution—is not simply a sprinkling of pixie dust; many harsh realities remain. But neither does the play mire itself in pessimism. Instead Caleb Lewis has opened the play to a more hopeful outlook, reminding us that, while social interactions may expose us to the abuse of power or burden us with debt and obligation, we can at least understand this dynamic and name it for what it is. For only then will true generosity—both in the giving and receiving—have a chance.

Murray Bramwell
Adelaide
June 2015

Murray Bramwell is an Adelaide-based reviewer and an adjunct Associate Professor in Drama at Flinders University.

Writer's Notes

I'm interested in the tension between economics and culture. How transactional have our relationships become? How do borrowing and lending affect our relationships with others? How much are we willing to lend and to borrow—how deep in someone else's debt are we willing to fall.

This is a play about the politics of charity and the sometimes complex motives behind altruism. Is it better for the soul to give or to receive? How does this affect our relationships with others and our own sense of self? Once in someone else's debt is it possible to remain equals or is one forever beholden? And once obligated how far will we go to clear our debt, or conversely to reclaim what's ours? How does debt shape our lives? And where does morality sit on this ledger?

Secondly, I was curious about the lives of our newest neighbours. In recent years Australia has welcomed thousands of migrants from the Sudan. For many their integration has not been easy. Often maligned in the media, few realise the immense trauma and hardship these people have suffered. Many have endured terribly at home and in the long journey to our shores, a place where many face new discrimination, prejudice and fear. Recent arrivals face a world of possibility and new beginnings but also one in which they are hopelessly, inescapably visible as 'Other'. Life here may be better but there is much to learn and the past still haunts. The journey is not over.

For several years, volunteering with the excellent not-for-profit organisation, SAIL (Sudanese Australian Integrated Learning) in Blacktown, I was struck again and again by the optimism, generosity and humour of the women I met. This play is dedicated to them.

Thanks to Adam Cook for commissioning the play and to Geordie Brookman for programming it. Thanks also to Catherine Fitzgerald and Suzie Miller for their insightful dramaturgy and to all actors involved in the play's development. Lastly thanks to the incredible Kris McQuade and the rest of the brilliant cast and crew who helped bring this complicated woman and her world to life.

Caleb Lewis

*'Everything costs. Everything has a price.
We learn to live in the balance.'*

Maggie Stone was commissioned and first produced by State Theatre Company of South Australia. at the Space Theatre, Adelaide, on 8 November 2013 with the following cast:

MAGGIE STONE	Kris McQuade
PROSPER DENG / BENEDICT DENG	Shedrick Yarkpai
AMATH DENG	Sara Zwangobani
GEORGINA SPACK	Genevieive Mooy
LEO HERMES	Mark Saturno
MAHIRA SADAT / DOCTOR	Ansuya Nathan

Director, Geordie Brookman
Set Designer, Victoria Lamb
Costume Designer, Olivia Zanchetta
Lighting Designer, Chris Petridis
Composer/Sound Designer, Andrew Howard
Assistant Director, Charles Sanders

CHARACTERS

    MAGGIE STONE, female, mid 50s, a loans officer
    PROSPER DENG, male, mid 30s, a meat packer
    AMATH DENG, female, mid 30s, a carer
    GEORGINA SPACK, female, late 50s, retired
    BENEDICT (BENNY) DENG, male, 17, a student
    LEO HERMES, male, early 50s, in micro-finance
    MAHIRA SADAT, female, 40s, owns a middle-eastern grocery store
    DOCTOR, female

A cast of six. Prosper and Benedict are both played by the same actor. Mahira Sadat should also double as the Doctor.

NOTATION

/	indicates the next line begins at this point, overlapping.
—	indicates the next line interrupts and cuts off this line.
…	at the end of a speech indicates it trails off. On it's own it suggests a pressure, expectation or desire to speak.
(…)	bracketed dialogue suggests an unspoken intention or thought.
Example	smaller font indicates the line should be whispered or muttered.

ACT ONE: A LOAN

There was a jolly miller once lived on the River Dee
He worked and sang from morn to night
No lark so blithe as he
And this, the burden of his song
Was ever wont to be—
I care for nobody, no, not I
And nobody cares for me...

                                    Traditional English folk song

SCENE ONE

A bank. Maggie Stone's office. Lunch-time. A laptop on the desk.
MAGGIE *is seated behind a desk. She holds a bin.*
PROSPER DENG *stands in the doorway, dressed in a pair of black trousers and a white shirt. He carries a green Coles shopping bag.*

MAGGIE: Here. [*Beat.*] In the hopper out back.

   He continues smiling, waiting.

Fucksake.

   She calls him over with a finger.

In. The bin. Out. Side.

   PROSPER *nods, embarrassed. He exits.*

   MAGGIE *clutches her chest, groans, searches her pockets, takes out a Quick-Eze heartburn relief tablet, chews it, washes it down with a swig from her hip flask. Another for good measure. She puts the bottle away, takes out a greasy burger and chips. About to bite when...*

   PROSPER *re-enters with the empty bin.*

Leave it there.

   PROSPER *places the bin. Waits.*

Can I help you?

PROSPER: Yes! Thank you!

    PROSPER *comes into the room, pumps her hand warmly.*

MAGGIE: And you are—
PROSPER: Prosper Deng
MAGGIE: Mr Deng—
PROSPER: Please call me Prosper. And you are Maggie Stone. Senior Loans Officer with—
MAGGIE: It's lunch time.
PROSPER: [*pointing at her hamburger*] Yes!
MAGGIE: *My* lunch time.
PROSPER: …
MAGGIE: Go clean the toilets.

    Beat.

PROSPER: Ms Stone. I think you are confused.
MAGGIE: *I'm* confused?!
PROSPER: A misunderstanding.
MAGGIE: Listen! You're the one who—

    She clocks the paperwork under his arm.

Oh.
You don't (work here)
The shirt—I thought—
I mean you look like—
PROSPER: Here is your bin.

    Beat.

MAGGIE: Thanks.
PROSPER: Let us begin again.
MAGGIE: Sure.
PROSPER: Excuse me—
MAGGIE: Oh, hello!
PROSPER: I am here for a loan.
MAGGIE: Great! Just pop in to Mandy two doors down.
PROSPER: Mandy is a very helpful woman.
MAGGIE: That's right.
PROSPER: She directed me to you!
MAGGIE: What? No, I'm sorry.

ACT ONE

PROSPER: I have references. This is from our landlord Mr Brennan / and our reverend at church. A very good man.
MAGGIE: You need to make an appointment.
> *He takes a seat.*

Mr Teng!
PROSPER: 'Deng'. It means rain.
> *She coolly regards him. Takes a bite out of her hamburger, chews it slowly, trying to get a gauge on him. He smiles, polite but firm. When she sips her Coke he starts to speak. She raises a finger. He waits. She takes another bite.* PROSPER *waits. When she is ready she opens up the laptop and types.*

MAGGIE: Occupation?
PROSPER: Sorry?
MAGGIE: Job. Do you have a—?
PROSPER: Meatpacking.
MAGGIE: How long have you—?
PROSPER: Three years.
MAGGIE: Almost a local.
PROSPER: … Not quite.
MAGGIE: Full-time? Part-time?
PROSPER: Casual.
MAGGIE: How many hours—?
PROSPER: It depends.
MAGGIE: Ballpark.
PROSPER: I'm sorry?
MAGGIE: Give me a ballpark figure.
PROSPER: I don't know this word.
MAGGIE: Last week.
PROSPER: I didn't work last week. My car. That's why I'm—
MAGGIE: The week before.
PROSPER: To fix my car. To drive to work.
MAGGIE: …
PROSPER: I think fifty.
MAGGIE: Think or—
PROSPER: Fifty.
MAGGIE: And how much do you earn?

PROSPER: 'At the ballpark'? Seven hundred.
MAGGIE: A week.
PROSPER: A fortnight.
MAGGIE: A fortnight?
PROSPER: Yes.
MAGGIE: I'll need to see payslips.
PROSPER: Payslips?
MAGGIE: You know, payslips.
PROSPER: They just give us the money.
MAGGIE: How much would you like to borrow?
PROSPER: Eight hundred.
MAGGIE: What for?
PROSPER: To spend.
MAGGIE: …
PROSPER: Oh, sorry! My English—
MAGGIE: To spend on what?
PROSPER: My car. The radiator is an orange.
MAGGIE: … Family?

    PROSPER *gets out his wallet. Takes out a photograph.*

PROSPER: My son, Benedict. Our baby daughter, Grace. Two weeks. And that beautiful woman there is my wife.
MAGGIE: Very nice. Does she work?
PROSPER: Thank you.
MAGGIE: Er—you're welcome. So she works?
PROSPER: Very hard.
MAGGIE: Where?
PROSPER: At home.
MAGGIE: What does she—?
PROSPER: Cooking, cleaning, / looking after the baby.
MAGGIE: No. That's not what—
PROSPER: And the shopping as well.
MAGGIE: I mean a job.
PROSPER: But she is a woman. [*Beat.*] In my culture. Women don't—
MAGGIE: Any other debts? Home loan, car loan, personal loan, credit cards.
PROSPER: I have a VISA.

ACT ONE

He hands it over.

MAGGIE: Never defaulted? I'll check.
PROSPER: When I first arrive in this country I did not know something called bills, I did not know how and when to pay them.

   MAGGIE *whistles.*

I've paid nearly all of it back.
MAGGIE: Expensive lesson.
PROSPER: They are the ones best learned.
MAGGIE: Ever been in prison?
PROSPER: I'm sorry?
MAGGIE: Locked up.
PROSPER: Detention?
MAGGIE: A comedian.
PROSPER: I really need this loan.
MAGGIE: And you promise to pay it all back.
PROSPER: Of course.

   Beat.

MAGGIE: I'm gonna do you a favour, Mr Deng.
PROSPER: [*shaking her hand vigorously*] You have saved my life!
MAGGIE: Alright, don't lay it on too thick.
PROSPER: [*still shaking her hand*] I was so worried I would lose my job.
MAGGIE: I think there's enough of you unemployed. Provided all your details check out we can have the money in your account by next week.
PROSPER: Next week? I really need it today.
MAGGIE: Ha!
PROSPER: Please—is there some way—?
MAGGIE: Sure. Ask Bob Geldof.
PROSPER: Does he work here?
MAGGIE: Not gonna happen.

   PROSPER *wrings his hands, moans.*

Mr Deng?
PROSPER: I HAVE TO WORK TOMORROW! [*Beat.*] It's across the other side of town. Yesterday I caught a taxi. It cost seventy dollars. I don't have any more money.
MAGGIE: So call in sick.

PROSPER: They will fire me!
MAGGIE: Okay. I don't think you should be telling me this.
PROSPER: If I don't earn the money by next week—
MAGGIE: What money?
PROSPER: …
MAGGIE: To fix your car?
PROSPER: …
MAGGIE: Mr Deng. What money?
PROSPER: …
MAGGIE: You told me you had no other debts.
PROSPER: …
MAGGIE: Which bank?
PROSPER: …
MAGGIE: CBA? National? Westpac?
PROSPER: … It's not a bank.
MAGGIE: Oh.

Beat.

PROSPER: He said if I missed another payment—
MAGGIE: Stop! You shouldn't be telling me this.
PROSPER: He will kill me.
MAGGIE: So call the police.

MAGGIE *sweeps up his paperwork and starts piling it back into his bag.*

PROSPER: Wait! The loan is approved? You said—

MAGGIE *hands the Coles bag back to him.*

I don't understand.
MAGGIE: I can't help you.
PROSPER: But—
MAGGIE: You already owe the bank money.
PROSPER: A few hundred.
MAGGIE: You've defaulted twice and now you want to borrow more? Why would we do that? Why would we give you more?
PROSPER: Yes. But a moment ago—
MAGGIE: I can't help you, Mr Deng.

Beat.

ACT ONE

PROSPER: You are killing me.
MAGGIE: The bank's position is clear.
PROSPER: Please. Without my car I am lost.
MAGGIE: That's not my problem.
PROSPER: …
MAGGIE: Now. If you'll excuse me—

    PROSPER *swears in Dinka.*

I beg your pardon?
PROSPER: …
MAGGIE: You people ask for more and more and it never makes a difference. But if we ever say no—
I can't help you.
PROSPER: That's not good enough!
MAGGIE: Good enough? You think the world owes you?! Just because you're— Let me give you some advice, Mr Deng.
PROSPER: What about my family? How do I look after them?

Kris McQuade as Maggie Stone and Shedrick Yarkpai as Prosper Deng in State Theatre Company of South Australia's 2013 production at the Space Theatre, Adelaide. (Photo: Matt Nettheim)

MAGGIE: Go out and mug someone. Isn't that what you people do?

Beat. PROSPER *rises. He takes his bag, walks away with great dignity.*

PROSPER: … I hope one day you will love someone more than yourself. And if something happens and you can no longer protect them—I hope you meet someone kinder than you.

PROSPER *exits.*

SCENE TWO

Maggie's flat.

MAGGIE *is alone eating Chinese takeout, watching 'Today Tonight' on television. The topic is African crime gangs.*

Noise of a family above. Laughter. Kids screaming. Hindi music. Joyful chaos. The thud of kids running down the hall below.

MAGGIE *looks up resentfully, turns up the TV, tries to concentrate.*

The noise increases.

MAGGIE *sighs, gets a broom, bangs on the floor. Hard. This is a practised move.*

Laughter, muffled. The sound abates.

MAGGIE *picks up the TV remote, turns up the volume.*

SCENE THREE

Respite. Col's room. MAGGIE *talks to her brother, Col, unseen.*

MAGGIE: Big one last night. Few of the girls from work. We went out drinking and ended up at mine. You shoulda seen us, up on Dad's table, murdering Lady Gaga. We even had the curries upstairs banging on the ceiling. You woulda loved it.

I'm on my last warning at work… Gareth called me in for a talk. He said I need to work on my customer service. Can you believe it? Little prick. Barely off his own mum's tit and now he's riding mine.

I had a fella in yesterday. Black. Needed money to fix his car. I could have approved it. It was only eight hundred.

…

Not a bloody cent.

ACT ONE

> LEO *enters with a bunch of daffodils.*

LEO: Maggie?
MAGGIE: Leo?

> *Beat.* MAGGIE *makes to duck past him.*

LEO: Don't go!

> *He reaches out, she flinches, he notices, steps back. Awkward.*

How is he?
MAGGIE: What do you think?
LEO: Look at those whiskers. I'll give him a shave.
MAGGIE: The nurse can do it.
LEO: I don't mind.
MAGGIE: Makes no difference to him.

> *Beat.*

LEO: You look well.
MAGGIE: I don't.
LEO: It's nice to / see you
MAGGIE: How's Tracy?
LEO: Good. She's— You should come over.
MAGGIE: I'm busy.
LEO: Well, when you're—
MAGGIE: Daffodils?
LEO: Brighten up the room a bit.
MAGGIE: For who?
LEO: …
MAGGIE: They're only gonna die.
LEO: Mags—
MAGGIE: You shouldn't have.
LEO: We're family.
MAGGIE: You're not.
LEO: … I don't know how you stand it. This place is fucking depressing.
MAGGIE: It's a hospice.
LEO: Let me put him back in private.
MAGGIE: We tried that.
LEO: Let me help.
MAGGIE: We're fine.
LEO: Mags. I owe him.

MAGGIE: Yeah. You do.

MAGGIE *exits.*

SCENE FOUR

The bank. Maggie's office. AMATH, GEORGINA *and* MAGGIE. *Beat.*

MAGGIE: It's just—when you made your appointment—
GEORGINA: For Amath.
MAGGIE: I thought—
GEORGINA: I know. [*Winking at* AMATH] I'm afraid we've been quite cheeky.
MAGGIE: Right.
GEORGINA: Not every bank has been so helpful.
MAGGIE: ... Mrs Spack, I assure you—
GEORGINA: Yes. Everybody does.

Impasse.

MAGGIE: Is she working?
GEORGINA: Why don't you ask her?
MAGGIE: [*to* AMATH] Are you—?
AMATH: Yes.
MAGGIE: I see. And how long have you—?
GEORGINA: / Six months.
AMATH: A week. [*Beat.*] A week.
GEORGINA: Oh. Has it only been—?
MAGGIE: How much / do you earn? Per annum.
GEORGINA: Twenty-four thousand.

MAGGIE *looks to* AMATH *to confirm.* AMATH *nods.*

MAGGIE: Are you married?

AMATH *looks to* GEORGINA.

It's not a difficult question.
AMATH: ... My husband—
GEORGINA: He passed away. [*Beat.*] Terrible business.
Of course it's hard enough for any migrant—finding a house, a job, learning new life skills. Not to mention the cultural—
MAGGIE: I'm sorry, who are you?

ACT ONE

GEORGINA: We go to church together.
MAGGIE: Of course.
GEORGINA: I'm here to help.
MAGGIE: [*to* AMATH] Lucky you.

    AMATH *smiles*.

Any dependents?
GEORGINA: She means—
AMATH: Two.
MAGGIE: And how much would you like to borrow?
GEORGINA: We thought five / might be—
AMATH: Ten thousand.
GEORGINA: Amath, we decided—
AMATH: You decided!

    Beat.

MAGGIE: Ten thousand?
AMATH: …
MAGGIE: What for?
AMATH: Grace. My daughter.
GEORGINA: Six weeks.
AMATH: And also… [*She takes out a list.*] A car. A washing machine. My son's schoolbooks. And to send / back home.
GEORGINA: Amath!
MAGGIE: To Africa?
GEORGINA: She means—
MAGGIE: Shhh!
AMATH: What does it matter what I do with it?
MAGGIE: Because. If I approve you and you go all 'World Vision' on us and then default on the loan, that's my neck on the block. So before I stick it out—on *your* behalf—I get to ask a few questions. Fair?
AMATH: Eight thousand.

    Beat.

MAGGIE: Two
AMATH: Six.
MAGGIE: Bossy one, aren't you? Why don't we try for three?

    AMATH *nods.*

That's for you. Not all of bloody Rwanda.

GEORGINA: The Sudan.

> MAGGIE *starts entering details on the laptop.*

Ooh, I know! Why don't we make it an even five?
AMATH: Georgina.
MAGGIE: Five is an odd number.
GEORGINA: I know.
MAGGIE: Two's even…
Or we could borrow under *your* name?
GEORGINA: My name?
MAGGIE: Sure.
GEORGINA: But—
MAGGIE: If you really want to help?
GEORGINA: … Of course.
MAGGIE: Then it's settled.
GEORGINA: It's just—
MAGGIE: [*to* AMATH] Ten thousand, was it?
GEORGINA: That sounds complicated.
MAGGIE: Nothing to it.
GEORGINA: We don't have much time.
MAGGIE: I've got the form right here.
GEORGINA: Really that won't be necessary!
MAGGIE: Three thousand then. What's your name?
AMATH: Deng. Amath Deng.

> MAGGIE *stops. Closes her eyes. Beat.*

GEORGINA: It means rain. [*Beat.*] Are you alright?
MAGGIE: 'Course.
GEORGINA: You don't look—
MAGGIE: I'M FINE! [*Beat.*] Address.
AMATH: Eight Acacia Court, Richmond.
MAGGIE: Postcode?
AMATH: 5033.
MAGGIE: Your husband—
GEORGINA: I don't see what that / has to do with—
MAGGIE: Shhh! What was his name?
AMATH: Prosper. Prosper Deng.

> *Beat.*

ACT ONE 13

GEORGINA: Who's your manager?
AMATH: Georgina!
GEORGINA: I don't like your attitude.
MAGGIE: I'm sorry.
GEORGINA: [*rising*] No you're not.
AMATH: Sit down.
GEORGINA: We're leaving.
AMATH: No.
MAGGIE: Wait.
GEORGINA: [*to* MAGGIE] I don't have to take this.
AMATH: The money?! Why not?
MAGGIE: Mrs Spack.
GEORGINA: We're going.
AMATH: But—
GEORGINA: Amath, now!

> AMATH *looks at* GEORGINA *helplessly. Then to* MAGGIE. *Both women exit. Beat.* MAGGIE *pops another Quick-Eze, chews it down, swallows.*

END OF ACT ONE

ACT TWO: BLACK

Forgive us our debts as we forgive our debtors
> *Lord's Prayer*
> *King James Version*

SCENE ONE

The Deng home. A modest two-bedroom Housing Trust home in Richmond.
MAGGIE *stands in the doorway, an envelope in her hand.* AMATH *nurses Grace, guarded, unsure.*

MAGGIE: You've been approved.
AMATH: …
MAGGIE: Your loan.

> AMATH *doesn't move.*

Something wrong?
AMATH: How do you know where I live?
MAGGIE: Your application… [*Beat.*] Also I managed to bump it to four.
AMATH: Four thousand?

> AMATH *reaches for it.* MAGGIE *lowers it.*

MAGGIE: I just need you to sign.
AMATH: Sign?
MAGGIE: To say you received it.

> *Beat.*

AMATH: The loan is approved?
MAGGIE: Of course.
AMATH: But.
MAGGIE: What?
AMATH: I thought it was cancelled?
MAGGIE: No.
AMATH: Georgie said—
MAGGIE: Why would we cancel it?

ACT TWO

AMATH: She said you'd been—

She reaches for her mobile.

MAGGIE: Forget it. [*She turns for the door.*] I'm tryna do you a favour. If you don't want it—

AMATH: Wait! [*Beat.*] Please. Come in.

They step inside. The house is cramped but tidy.

Excuse the mess.

MAGGIE: This is nothing. Me and Trev live in a block filled with Indians. The place stinks!
… I meant the cooking.

Beat.

AMATH: Trev?

MAGGIE: Trevor.

AMATH: Have a seat.

MAGGIE sits.

MAGGIE: Now. I just need you to— Where ya going?

AMATH: It is time for her nap.

AMATH exits, leaving her handbag on the table next to an open photo album. A handle is sticking out of the handbag. MAGGIE *touches it. She pulls out a kitchen knife.* AMATH *re-enters without Grace.*

I could kill him!

MAGGIE thrusts the knife back into the bag and feigns interest in the photo album. AMATH *is oblivious.*

My son. His room is a mess.

MAGGIE points to a photo in the album.

MAGGIE: Is that him?
Oh, Jesus, that's—
Sorry.

AMATH: That was when we first met. In the camp in Kakuma.

MAGGIE: You sound like you miss it.

AMATH: Africa?

MAGGIE: …

AMATH: My husband, he never spoke of anything else. He missed his friends, his job. But these things, they weren't true. He only remembered the laugh. Not the ache...
Here there is everything.
MAGGIE: Just so long as you can pay for it.
AMATH: Yes.
MAGGIE: Here's a pen.

AMATH *takes the pen, about to sign, when...*

AMATH: Trevor is your husband?
MAGGIE: Me?! Married?! Ha! Trev's a blue-tongue lizard. You know, like a snake?
AMATH: A snake?!
MAGGIE: With legs.
AMATH: I hate snakes.
MAGGIE: These are nice.
AMATH: If you say so.
MAGGIE: I just need your signature here and—
AMATH: What does it say?
MAGGIE: Oh, the usual.
'I Amath Deng accept four thousand dollars etcetera etcetera'—
AMATH: ... 'wish to retract my earlier'—
MAGGIE: Ignore that, it's just a bunch of—

MAGGIE *attempts to snatch the contract away but* AMATH *holds it fast.*

AMATH: ... 'ask the bank to halt all proceedings against Ms Stone.' [*Beat.*] What is this?
MAGGIE: ... [*Beat.*] I've had two warnings. If I get one more...

The phone rings.

Four thousand dollars. That's a lot of...

The phone rings.

Look. I didn't come here to beg. Do you want it or not?

The phone rings.

The phone rings.

The phone rings.

AMATH: Eight.
MAGGIE: Five.
AMATH: Eight.

> *Beat.* MAGGIE *nods.* AMATH *picks up the phone. She speaks in Dinka*:*

*Hello?

*Where?

*Benny, what have I told you?! You must leave there at once!

*Why not?

*Are you in trouble?

*What have you done?!

*Benny?

*Hello? Benny!

> *The conversation grows more agitated. We hear Benny's name several times. She hangs up. Beat.*

MAGGIE: Everything okay?
AMATH: No, it is not okay.
MAGGIE: Can I do anything?

> AMATH *regards her coolly. Beat.*

AMATH: Do you have a car?

SCENE TWO

Happy Time Minimart. It's a mess.

BENEDICT DENG *(*BENNY*), wearing hip-hop gear and bling, is on the ground, nursing his ankle.* MAHIRA SADAT, *brandishing a mop.*

A bell as the shop door opens. AMATH *enters.*

BENNY: Mum!
AMATH: Benny!

> AMATH *rushes to her son, holds his face in her hands, checking him over.*

You are hurt?
BENNY: I'm okay.

> AMATH *starts beating him, abusing him in Dinka. He tries to fend her off.*

Mum! Stop! I didn't do anything.
AMATH: Why are you here? Why do you harass this woman?
BENNY: She harassed me!
MAHIRA: That is a lie! Look what he did to our store!
BENNY: You broke my ankle!
MAHIRA: He fell!
BENNY: She was chasing me with the mop!
MAHIRA: He wouldn't leave!
BENNY: She called me a thief!
MAHIRA: I tell you this is the last time! Next time I call the police!

> *The bell.* MAGGIE *enters.* BENNY *is obscured by* AMATH. *Everyone stops.*

[*To* MAHIRA] I'm with them.
BENNY: [*to* AMATH] Let's go.
MAHIRA: Oh no you don't.

> BENNY *tries to get to his feet.* MAGGIE *sees him. Stops. Like she's seen a ghost.*

Look, look what he did! Every day the boy comes here. He never buys anything.
BENNY: It's a free country.
MAHIRA: Not for all of us!
BENNY: Go back to Iraq!
AMATH: Benedict!
MAHIRA: I'm from Syria.
BENNY: Fucking Arab!
AMATH: What has come over you?
MAHIRA: You see this disrespect? All the time he is in here, watching, waiting for an opportunity.
BENNY: To what?
MAHIRA: I know who you are, boy!
BENNY: So?
MAHIRA: The apple doesn't fall far from the tree.

> BENNY *lunges at her, collapses on the floor. He cries out in rage. Beat.*

MAGGIE: Peas.

ACT TWO

MAHIRA: Sorry?
MAGGIE: Frozen peas. Got 'em?
MAHIRA: In the fridge.

> *Beat. Standoff.* MAHIRA *nods. Gets the peas. Returns.*

Five dollars.

> MAGGIE *takes out a fiver. She tosses one bag to* BENNY.

MAGGIE: For your ankle.

> BENNY *looks at her like she's crazy. Starts to open it.* AMATH *stops him, presses the bag to his ankle.* MAGGIE *holds out the fiver.* MAHIRA *takes it.* MAGGIE *holds on to it.*

Now, what happened?
BENNY: I didn't touch her!
MAHIRA: This is none of your concern.
MAGGIE: How much for the damages?
MAHIRA: I should call the police.
AMATH: No, please!
MAHIRA: First his father then the son. What sort of family—?

> BENNY *lunges again.*

AMATH: Benedict!
MAGGIE: Here.

> MAGGIE *offers her mobile phone. Everyone stops.*

Call them. Get them poking around, taking statements…
Most of us, we want to support local business but also we want to feel safe. We pop in for milk and a pack of ciggies, not little Beirut.
MAHIRA: Are you finished?
MAGGIE: … Then there's your insurance.
MAHIRA: We are covered.
MAGGIE: Still there's the excess. And your premium. That'll take a hit.
MAHIRA: …
MAGGIE: OR we can fix this ourselves.

> MAGGIE *takes out a cheque book.*

AMATH: Maggie?
MAGGIE: Shall we say one hundred?

Beat.

MAHIRA: A thousand.
MAGGIE: That's funny.
MAHIRA: Eight hundred.
MAGGIE: One twenty.
MAHIRA: Six. That is my final offer.
MAGGIE: The boy can sue, you know. His ankle.
MAHIRA: A sprain!
MAGGIE: In *your* store.
MAHIRA: His word against mine.
MAGGIE: With me as his witness.

Beat.

MAHIRA: Four.
MAGGIE: One.
MAHIRA: One fifty.
MAGGIE: Any Port Royal?
MAHIRA: Tobacco?
MAGGIE: I'll take a bag of that too. Now. Who do I make this out to?
MAHIRA: Mahira Sadat.
MAGGIE: M…
MAHIRA: A.H.I.R.A
MAGGIE: Sadat?
MAHIRA: Sadat. [*Beat.*] S.A.D.A.T.
MAGGIE: [*handing* MAHIRA *the cheque*] Amath, help Benny out to the car.
BENNY: Who are you?
AMATH: She works at the bank.

MAGGIE *hands* MAHIRA *a business card.*

MAGGIE: Here's my card. You see him in here again, you call me.
MAHIRA: That boy needs to learn!
MAGGIE: Oh, he'll learn alright.
   I don't believe in charity.
   [*Loud enough for* BENNY *to hear*] He's gonna pay me back every bloody cent.

SCENE THREE

Hospital. Col's room.

MAGGIE: Listen, I can't come next Saturday. I've been invited out. Lunch.
I probably won't go. I've got to go to the laundromat and I was gonna watch the game. They said bring nothing but you always have to bring something and it's across the other side of town.
I thought I might get my hair done.
If I go.
Which I won't.

SCENE FOUR

The Deng house. Day. Music is playing. Lively African dance. A table is set for dinner.

MAGGIE: Here.

    MAGGIE *thrusts the gift into* AMATH*'s hands.*

AMATH: You shouldn't have.
MAGGIE: It's for Grace.

    AMATH *opens it. A plastic piggy bank.*

AMATH: A pig?
MAGGIE: We get them free at the bank. Oh, and—

    MAGGIE *hands over a bottle of wine.*

AMATH: You look nice.
MAGGIE: Mutton dressed as lamb.
AMATH: Chicken.
MAGGIE: Sorry?
AMATH: With Kisra and stew.
MAGGIE: No—I meant—
AMATH: ?
MAGGIE: Yum.

    AMATH *smiles.*

Is Benny home?

AMATH: He is out with friends.

MAGGIE: Just us girls, hey?

> *The sound of a toilet flushing.* GEORGINA *enters.*

GEORGINA: Amath, I think there's a problem with your toilet, it won't— Oh? Hello.

AMATH: You remember Georgie.

MAGGIE: …

GEORGINA: [*ebullient*] Here she is, the woman of the hour! I hear you strolled in like John Wayne with a cheque book!

AMATH: Can you believe it? What a friend she has been.

GEORGINA: A regular fairy godmother.

MAGGIE: That's me.

GEORGINA: Ah… [*Taking the wine*] Do you mind? Amath doesn't drink.

> *She takes glasses from the cupboard and pours out drinks. She is familiar here.*

AMATH: Lunch will be soon.

GEORGINA: It smells divine.

> *She offers a glass of wine.*

Maggie?

MAGGIE: I might pop outside for a smoke.

GEORGINA: Yes, let's.

> GEORGINA *leads her out.*
>
> *The driveway.* MAGGIE *takes out her papers to roll a cigarette. Beat.*

Bygones be bygones…

MAGGIE: What?

GEORGINA: The whole complaint thing.

> MAGGIE *focuses on rolling.*

Of course I've withdrawn it.

MAGGIE: …

> GEORGINA *laughs awkwardly.*
>
> *Beat.*

ACT TWO 23

GEORGINA: Housing Trust.
MAGGIE: What?
GEORGINA: It's not much. But they were lucky to get it. She hasn't had it easy. Poor thing.
MAGGIE: She's doing alright.
GEORGINA: She's going broke. The husband borrowed from family to raise her dowry. Now he's gone it falls to Amath to pay it back.
MAGGIE: For her own dowry?
GEORGINA: The money's still owed. May I?

> MAGGIE *shrugs, hands over the smoke. Lights it for her. Starts on another one.*

MAGGIE: Doesn't she have friends?
GEORGINA: Of course.
But since her husband—she's withdrawn from everyone.
Even her own community.
If it weren't for me—
AMATH: [*from inside*] Five more minutes.
GEORGINA: [*calling out*] Take your time, darling. [*Beat.*] Of course the son is a lost cause. I give him a year before he ends up in prison.
MAGGIE: He just lost his dad.
GEORGINA: But her. What a survivor!
My husband says, what about the Greeks? The Vietnamese? They came out with nothing, they found work, they fit in—but it's different. Don't you think?
We're just so lucky. You know my husband owns a chain of carwashes. I only work one day a week. Just to feel useful. I have everything I could ever want and it makes me feel so *helpless*.
MAGGIE: I can imagine.
GEORGINA: Catholic, right?
MAGGIE: Guilty.
GEORGINA: And a wit as well!

> MAGGIE *draws on her fag.*

You and I rather got off on the wrong foot… I'd like us to be friends.

> MAGGIE *clutches her chest, bites down.*

Are you okay?

MAGGIE: She's got a knife in her bag.

>   *Beat.*

GEORGINA: I thought she'd stopped that.
MAGGIE: You know?
GEORGINA: …You have to understand. Where she's from—even in the camps people are starving. It's supposed to be safe but—
MAGGIE: What about the guards?
GEORGINA: They're the worst.
MAGGIE: Whole place is a mess.
GEORGINA: [*nodding*] That's why we have to give more.
MAGGIE: More?
GEORGINA: [*nodding*] Africa is teetering on the brink. They've seen *more* wars than—
MAGGIE: Oh, grow up!
GEORGINA: I beg your pardon?
MAGGIE: They're fighting for the aid! Whoever's in power gets the money. No wonder they're all staging coups. It's like musical chairs.
GEORGINA: So what? We do nothing?
MAGGIE: Five bucks a week isn't gonna fix it.
GEORGINA: …
MAGGIE: Look. You can piss down a well all your life but you'll never fill it. Some holes go too deep.

>   *Beat.*

GEORGINA: The world must look so ugly to you.

>   GEORGINA *finishes smoking, stubs her cigarette out and turns to go back inside.*

MAGGIE: Remember that cartoon?
The one about the ant and the grasshopper. And all summer long the grasshopper's having a lark, not a care in the world. And meanwhile the ant is slaving its guts out. But the ant knows winter is on its way. And when it does, sure enough, who comes knocking on the door? I woulda let that prick starve.
AMATH: [*from inside*] COME AND EAT IT!

>   GEORGINA *exits back into the house.* MAGGIE *follows. Once inside…*

Have you two made up?

ACT TWO

GEORGINA: Oh, yes! We're like two peas in a pod. Only I think Maggie has to go.
AMATH: No! Why?
GEORGINA: Isn't it a shame?
AMATH: But you just got here.
GEORGINA: Now don't pressure her.
AMATH: Half an hour. / That's all.
GEORGINA: No, really, she has to—
MAGGIE: Alright, I'll stay.

Beat.

GEORGINA: Well… That's… Isn't that—?
MAGGIE: [*smelling*] Delicious.
GEORGINA: Yes. You'll have to give me the recipe.

They sit while AMATH *serves.*

Oh look, my old dinner set!
AMATH: It was very generous.

AMATH *goes on serving.*

GEORGINA: What's this?
AMATH: A gift from Maggie.
GEORGINA: A gift?!
AMATH: Grace will love it.
GEORGINA: Of course she's far too young now.
MAGGIE: It was that or a well.
GEORGINA: In this house, we don't joke about poverty.
AMATH: Georgie!
MAGGIE: I didn't know you lived here?

Beat. AMATH *serves lunch. She offers cutlery.*

GEORGINA: None for me thanks.
AMATH: Maggie?
GEORGINA: Have you eaten Kisra before?

MAGGIE *nods.*

Just tear it and dip into the stew. You're probably more used to McDonald's.

They eat in silence.

MAGGIE: Has Georgie told you? She's offered Benny a job.

GEORGINA *nearly chokes on her food.*

AMATH: Truly?

MAGGIE: At the carwash. After school.

GEORGINA: Oh, I—uh. Yes. Well, it's up to David of course.

MAGGIE: A technicality.

AMATH: Thank you.

MAGGIE: He starts Monday right?

GEORGINA: Maggie. Could I talk to you?

MAGGIE: To Saint George.

GEORGINA: / Georgina…

AMATH: Yes. St George.

GEORGINA: … to new friends.

Beat. They eat in silence.

So, Maggie. Is there someone special in your life?

MAGGIE: I'm between headaches.

GEORGINA: [*explaining to* AMATH] That means she's a spinster.

AMATH: Spin. Ster.

GEORGINA: An old maid.

She winks at MAGGIE. MAGGIE *would like to punch her in the head.*
MAGGIE reaches for the wine.

[*Slapping* MAGGIE*'s hand*] Uh-uh.

She takes the bottle and pours.

Say when.

A standoff. She nearly fills the glass before…

MAGGIE: When.

There's now just a trickle left for GEORGINA.

GEORGINA: Amath, can you get me a water?

AMATH *rises to get it.* GEORGINA *is fine with this. Beat.* MAGGIE *gulps her wine.* AMATH *returns.*

MAGGIE: [*to* AMATH] You got plans this week?

GEORGINA: As a matter of fact, I'm taking Amath and Grace to the clinic.

ACT TWO

AMATH: No, really.
GEORGINA: [*winking*] You owe me one.
MAGGIE: You always keep score?
GEORGINA: Oh, for goodness sake, it's a figure of speech.
MAGGIE: Then why bring it up?
AMATH: Do you like 'Home and Away'?
MAGGIE: Unless you want to remind her.
AMATH: / It is very good but I worry about Indigo. She should be with Romeo, that Brax is no good.

The following conversation runs over the top of AMATH.

GEORGINA: Remind her of what?
MAGGIE: How much she owes you.
GEORGINA: Oh, come on.
MAGGIE: How much you've invested in your little 'Rent-a-friend'!

GEORGINA *pushes her chair back, loudly, rises.*

From left: Kris McQuade as Maggie Stone, Sara Zwangobani as Amath Deng and Genevieve Mooy as Georgiina Spack in State Theatre Company of South Australia's 2013 production at the Space Theatre, Adelaide. (Photo: Matt Nettheim)

You said yourself. Her husband bought her like a slave. Her own family. They sold her for some fucking cows!

GEORGINA: You're drunk.

MAGGIE: I'm not.

GEORGINA: I think you should go.
Amath, call her a cab.
Amath!

Long beat. MAGGIE *finishes her meal in silence. She dabs at her face with a napkin, raises her wine. She gulps it down.* MAGGIE *rises. Heads for the door.*

MAGGIE: Thank you for a lovely…

She collapses on the floor.

SCENE FIVE

Hospital. MAGGIE *sits on the bed opposite* DOCTOR HASSAN.

MAGGIE: What happened to the other one?

DOCTOR: The other what?

MAGGIE: The other doctor.

DOCTOR: Which one?

MAGGIE: The one from before.

DOCTOR: I don't know.

MAGGIE: It's just—I thought I'd be talking to him.

DOCTOR: Him?

MAGGIE: …

DOCTOR: Does it matter?

MAGGIE: No.

It does.

DOCTOR: What did he look like?

MAGGIE: …

DOCTOR: Was he tall? Short? Fat? Thin?

MAGGIE: Blonde.

Beat.

DOCTOR: I see.
Doctor 'White' has gone home.

ACT TWO

MAGGIE: When will he be back?
DOCTOR: Tomorrow. In the meantime…
MAGGIE: I thought you all drove taxis. [*Aside*] I suppose that's just the men.
DOCTOR: … I'm afraid it's not good news.
MAGGIE: Hit me.
DOCTOR: Arteriosclerosis….

> DOCTOR *takes out a model heart.*

MAGGIE: Oh, you shouldn't have.
DOCTOR: Ms Stone, your heart is choking.
MAGGIE: Cholesterol.
DOCTOR: And numerous other fats. The build-up of plaque in your arteries is significant. It explains your chest pains, also the sweating, dizziness.
MAGGIE: I thought it was menopause.
DOCTOR: We can try to lower your blood pressure—that'll slow the build-up as well as lowering the risk of stroke… BUT… without a change in diet, exercise, your whole lifestyle—
MAGGIE: I'll wait for Dr White.
DOCTOR: No more take-away, no more cigarettes or alcohol.
MAGGIE: Pray to Allah.
DOCTOR: Ms Stone!
You had a heart attack. Even a minor one should be taken seriously. If you have any leave I recommend you take it. The important thing now is to rest. And avoid any stress. [*Pointing to* MAGGIE's *chest*] This won't take the strain.

> DOCTOR *is about to leave.* MAGGIE, *suddenly vulnerable, calls out after her.*

MAGGIE: Doctor?
DOCTOR: [*relenting*] … You have the heart of an ox. How it still beats, I don't know. But here you are.
MAGGIE: How long have I got?
DOCTOR: *Inshallah.*

> DOCTOR *exits leaving* MAGGIE *alone. Beat.* AMATH *enters, carrying a Tupperware container.*

AMATH: You gave us a scare.

MAGGIE: I'm fine.

> AMATH *looks at her questioningly then to the telltale heart.*

Be out tomorrow. Couple a weeks and I'll be right as rain.
AMATH: This is good news.
MAGGIE: Yeah, apparently I'm a hard-hearted bitch.

> AMATH *smiles.*

About yesterday—
AMATH: I brought more stew.
MAGGIE: I've just eaten.
AMATH: Then… [*Putting it down*] Perhaps later.
MAGGIE: You don't have to do this.
AMATH: Do you have someone to pick you up?
MAGGIE: I'll get a taxi.
AMATH: There's no-one you can ask?
MAGGIE: …
AMATH: What about Trevor?
MAGGIE: He can't drive.
AMATH: I meant someone to feed him. If you want / I can—
MAGGIE: I don't. [*Beat.*] Get Benny to. And tell him we're square.
AMATH: No. My son must learn.
MAGGIE: …
AMATH: He is a good boy. But—since his father… Now there is this anger inside him all the time.
MAGGIE: Kids are tough.
AMATH: But he doesn't understand. They say my husband is a thief, but he was a good man. He took me when no-one else would. He bought us ice-creams at Glenelg. We played mini-golf and he took us on the rides. This is the man I know. Not this other man. This thief. So we are hurting because we are confused.
MAGGIE: … What happened?
AMATH: They shot him.

> …

After he robbed that store.
They found him in the car.
Broken down on the side of the road.
They say he had a gun.

That he was waving it around.
Screaming.
But they couldn't understand…
And then.

She pauses, visibly upset. She takes a breath before continuing.

After.
They found the gun in the gutter.
A plastic pistol.
A toy.

Beat.

MAGGIE: It gets easier. I know people tell you that, but it's true. When my brother—
… It's a kick in the teeth.

AMATH picks up the heart, examining it.

AMATH: Before I come here. All my life is the neighbours. My parents were gone, my brothers missing. When I got married, neighbours help prepare the feast. When I had Benedict, neighbours help look after him. In Kakuma, neighbours are the most important thing. Because if there is a problem in the middle of the night, family cannot help, they are too far away. But the neighbour… Whoever the person who is close to you, you can call on for help. Understand?

MAGGIE: Listen… I had no right to say those things.

AMATH: But you think them.

MAGGIE: …

AMATH: That my husband bought me like a slave. That he took advantage. Here in the West you think you know everything. About what is best for everyone. But there are things you don't know…
Back in Kenya—in the camps—they say we can stay there for free. But everybody wants something. The journalists want our stories; the NGOs want us to sing in their choirs; the SPLA wants our sons as soldiers. The spirits of our ancestors want us to honour them…

She puts the heart down.

People think it is easy. To be helped. But it is hard. It takes courage. Don't you think?

MAGGIE: … I'll eat it tonight.

SCENE SIX

Amath's house. Evening.

AMATH, *in uniform, on her phone with* BENNY. *She speaks in Dinka, her voice frantic, angry.*

A knock at the door. It's MAGGIE. AMATH, *still talking agitatedly into the phone, ushers her inside.* MAGGIE *carries the empty Tupperware container in one hand, an exotic cushion in the other. She waits while* AMATH *finishes on the phone.*

MAGGIE: I'm just returning your container.

>AMATH *starts sending a text.*

The stew was lovely. Really.

AMATH: …

MAGGIE: Oh, and I found this at home. [*She produces the cushion.*] You don't like it? That's okay. I've still got the receipt.

AMATH: He's out all night. He sleeps all day!

MAGGIE: Who?

AMATH: My no-good son!

MAGGIE: Oh.

AMATH: He should have been home hours ago! He doesn't call or text. He doesn't answer his phone!

MAGGIE: Kids.

AMATH: He was supposed to mind Grace. I start work in twenty minutes! Now I will have to call someone from church.

MAGGIE: I'll do it.

>*Beat.*

AMATH: You?!

MAGGIE: I'm just sitting at home.

>*Beat.*

AMATH: … It wouldn't be long. Just a few hours…

MAGGIE: Go.

AMATH: You're sure?

MAGGIE: She can help me do my tax.

AMATH: You are a good friend.

ACT TWO   33

    AMATH *turns to go.*

MAGGIE: What do I do? If the baby wakes?
AMATH: Nurse her.

    She has her coat on, headed for the door.

    There is milk in the fridge.

MAGGIE: And if I see Benny?
AMATH: You may beat him for *me!*

    AMATH *darts back, pecks* MAGGIE *on the cheek and is out the door.*
    MAGGIE, *stunned, touches her cheek.*

SCENE SEVEN

The Deng house. Later that night. MAGGIE *is asleep on the couch, snoring.*

BENNY *enters. Goes to creep past, hears the snoring, looks at her quizzically, looks around for his mum. Stands there listening to her snore. Shrugs, starts for his room. He is nearly out of the room when his phone rings. He freezes, opens the phone right away and answers.*

BENNY: [*in a hushed voice*] Hello Sophie? Uh-huh. Mmhm. I can't talk… There is someone in our house. A white woman. On the couch. Sleeping. Old. And not as pretty as you.

    MAGGIE *snorts.*

[*Whispering*] I have to go.

    BENNY *hangs up, starts to creep out of the room.*

MAGGIE: [*eyes still closed*] Stop. Right. There.
BENNY: You're the lady from the bank.
MAGGIE: You're three hours late.
BENNY: Where's Mum?
MAGGIE: At work.
BENNY: Shit!
MAGGIE: She's not happy with you.
BENNY: Shit shit shit.
MAGGIE: Nice trainers.
BENNY: …
MAGGIE: How's the job going?

BENNY *shrugs.*

First pay packet, I see.

BENNY *scowls, pulls out his wallet and throws it at her. She looks at him, non-plussed, opens it.*

Thirty bucks!
BENNY: That's all I have left.

MAGGIE *takes out a pocket book, licks her finger, turns the page, writes.*

MAGGIE: Thirty-one dollars and forty cents. Paid on [*today's date*].
BENNY: At least leave ten for the bus!
MAGGIE: You can walk. Show off your new shoes.

She tosses his wallet back.

And next month I'd like the full fifty we agreed on, thanks.
BENNY: Can I go?
MAGGIE: Why were you harassing Mrs Sadat?
BENNY: …
MAGGIE: You're smarter than that.

BENNY *mutters under his breath in Dinka.*

Sorry, I don't speak gibberish. You're in Australia now.
BENNY: Fuck off.
MAGGIE: You're welcome.
BENNY: Am I?
MAGGIE: Here we go.
BENNY: You invite us here and then treat us like a pest. You tell us we're welcome yet you bar all your doors.
MAGGIE: People will start trusting you when you earn it.
BENNY: When I walk down the street at night—people are afraid. They think you are a thief. That you are going to bash them or worse.
MAGGIE: So stop dressing like Snoopy Dogg! Christ, don't you own any clothes that fit?! You could start with that.
BENNY: And my skin? What should I do about that?
MAGGIE: …
BENNY: They think we are animals. You don't know what that's like.

Beat.

MAGGIE: My brother was a thief. Break-ins, armed robbery, you name it. He was angry like you. Thought he was a hard man.
But when he tried to quit he'd left it too late. The violence was in him now, always looking for a way out. Until he met some people harder. I saw him after. The fire in his eyes had been pissed on. Now there's nothing left but mud.
The road you're on. My brother went down it. You're not strong enough. It'll snap you in two.

BENNY dismisses her, about to leave.

And your mum? How d'you think she'd cope?

He stops.

Well?

BENNY: I thought if I talked to her...

MAGGIE: Who?

BENNY: The woman at the store... She was the last person who saw my dad alive.
...
I wanted to ask her... But when I got in there, the way she looked at me, it made me so angry.

Beat. He nods. A moment of recognition between them. Then...

MAGGIE: Who's Sophie?

BENNY: What?

MAGGIE: Is she pretty?

BENNY smiles.

Are you blushing?

BENNY: No!

MAGGIE: I can't tell.

They are laughing.

BENNY: You are a racist!

MAGGIE: You ask her out yet?

BENNY: I can't afford it.
Mum takes all my youth allowance to send to family back home. I need a new uniform, a laptop, but none of that matters. We send everything to some aunty or cousin I've never even met.

Beat.

MAGGIE: Here.

She holds out the thirty dollars.

Take her to the movies.

BENNY: Really?

MAGGIE: But I want double next month.

BENNY *nods, takes it.*

BENNY: Have you ever been married?

MAGGIE: Me? No. I never met the right man…

BENNY: That is very sad.

MAGGIE: How much you pay for those shoes?

BENNY: Ninety dollars.

MAGGIE: Now that's sad!

BENNY *laughs.*

Your mum. She coulda dropped me in the shit. But she didn't.

BENNY: …

MAGGIE: I don't like owing people.

I'm not good at it.

SCENE EIGHT

The Beach House, Glenelg (formerly Magic Mountain).

Lights. Noise. Sounds of video games. Funhouse tunes. Pop music. A cacophony of sound.

AMATH *and* BENNY *are arguing fiercely in Dinka.* BENNY *is upset.* AMATH *attempts to calm him.*

In Dinka*:

*BENNY: I don't want to be here.

*AMATH: Benny, I know.

*BENNY: Why has she brought us here?

*AMATH: She thinks she is helping.

*BENNY: She is not!

*AMATH: She thinks we will like this.

*BENNY: Do you?

ACT TWO

*AMATH: Of course not!
*BENNY: So tell her!

    MAGGIE *enters holding three ice-creams.*

MAGGIE: Here we go. Also I've got passes for the waterslide and ride vouchers.
BENNY: Fucking unbelievable!
AMATH: Benny!
MAGGIE: You should have seen this place before. Looked like a big turd laid right on the beach. Magic bloody Mountain!
Right! Who's up for dodgems?
*BENNY: Say something.
*AMATH: In a moment.
BENNY: Tell her!
AMATH: Shhh.
MAGGIE: Tell me what? [*Beat.*] Hello?
BENNY: What is this?
MAGGIE: Hokey pokey.
BENNY: Fucking—
AMATH: This is very generous—
BENNY: I want to leave.
MAGGIE: Why? [*Beat.*] I've already bought the vouchers.
AMATH: This is where we came as a family.
MAGGIE: I know. I thought—

    BENNY *swears in Dinka. He throws his ice-cream on the ground and storms off.*

Hey!

    He stops.

BENNY: YOU ARE NOT MY DAD!

    He stalks off. MAGGIE *starts after him.*

AMATH: Maggie! Let him be.

    Beat. They eat their ice-creams in silence.

MAGGIE: Kid needs a good kick up his arse.
AMATH: It hasn't been easy. Ever since Prosper…
MAGGIE: I know.

AMATH: But then you came, like a guardian angel / into our lives.
MAGGIE: No, I only—
AMATH: Please. Let me speak.
MAGGIE: …
AMATH: You have been a good friend to us. Like a big sister.
MAGGIE: …
AMATH: But you are not my sister.
MAGGIE: …
AMATH: So we ask, why does she help us? And what does she want in return?
MAGGIE: Nothing!
I thought we were friends.
AMATH: We are.
MAGGIE: Then why are you asking me—?
AMATH: Because I must.
MAGGIE: Unbelievable.
The fucken ingratitude.
I try to do something nice for you and you throw it back in my face. Well, go on. Piss off then. I'll have the ice-cream back too.

    MAGGIE *snatches* AMATH*'s ice-cream.* AMATH *turns to go.*

Wait! [*Beat.*] Here.

    MAGGIE *holds out the ice-cream. Beat.*

Go on, take it. I don't even like spearmint.
AMATH: What do you want from us?
MAGGIE: I said. Nothing.
AMATH: Why are we here?
MAGGIE: Are you deaf? I said—

    AMATH *turns to leave.*

My brother!
He came to me and I…
I hadn't seen him in years then one night he just shows up at my door and expects me to—
I *knew* I wouldn't get the money back.
AMATH: How much did you lend him?
MAGGIE: … Nothing. [*Beat.*] Please, will you take the bloody—
It's dripping down my arm.

Beat. AMATH *takes the ice-cream.*

AMATH: What happened to your brother?

MAGGIE: None of your *fucking business!* [*She is visibly upset.*] Why was your husband doing hold-ups? I mean, how fucken dumb.

AMATH: You are right.

People said he was generous, my husband, like it is always a good thing. But this thing came from pride—so everyone would say, 'Ah, Prosper Deng. What a success!' And when they asked to borrow money, always he said yes. He took on two jobs, then three, and when that wasn't enough he gambled, and when he lost then he borrowed and when the banks turned him down...

He borrowed from one crook to pay off another. He thought it would never catch up with him. And then one day... [*Beat.*] Everybody loved him. And from the moment we met he adored me.

MAGGIE: Love at first sight.

AMATH: No. I wanted something better.

MAGGIE: ... Then— (why marry him?)

AMATH: Who else would have me?

MAGGIE: But you're beautiful.

AMATH: ...

MAGGIE: I mean—

AMATH: My sister. She was such a flirt. Always smiling, batting her eyes. All the men wanted her. One of the guards, a Kenyan, he was so handsome, always he offers to help, always he is bringing gifts and always she said yes.

One evening we were searching for firewood when the men approached. Four other guards and the Kenyan.

...

My sister died that night. How I survived I do not know.

Prosper found me.

And after. After I missed my blood twice and no-one else would touch me, he married me. He borrowed from friends and family to raise the dowry and he took me for his wife and raised Benny as his son when no-one else would. My sister. She was not careful...

Nothing is free.

Someone always pays the price.

SCENE NINE

The Deng house. Driveway. Night. The house lights are out.

AMATH *and* BENNY *and* MAGGIE *arrive home. They are laughing.*

MAGGIE: So this customer wanted to take out equity on his home.
AMATH: What is equity?
BENNY: Fairness.
MAGGIE: No! What do they teach you in school?! It's the value of the property. So I say to him, what's your house worth? And he says, I don't know. I RENT!

   Beat.

AMATH: I don't get it.
MAGGIE: Ah, forget it.

   They get the door open. Switch the lights on. The house has been trashed. All the electrical goods are gone, windows broken, the door kicked in. They freeze.

   A message spray-painted on the wall: 'THE BALANCE IS DUE'.

END OF ACT TWO

ACT THREE: THE DEFICIENCY

Morality is the way people would like the world to work; economics is the way it does work.

Stephen Levitt

SCENE ONE

A pawn shop.

LEO *is messing with a new mobile phone. He can't get the alarm off. It sounds out endlessly.*

A bell as MAGGIE *enters.*

LEO: Fucking shitfuck piece of— [*Looking up*] Maggie?
MAGGIE: 'Lo Leo.
LEO: Col?!
MAGGIE: He's fine.
 Beat.
LEO: Tracy got it for me. Thing needs a fucking pilot's licence.
MAGGIE: Here.
LEO: Don't waste your time, I've tried every—
 MAGGIE *switches it off.*
 Oh.
 She hands it back.
 So your brother's—
MAGGIE: Still dribbling.
LEO: ... If you've changed your mind, about putting him in private.
MAGGIE: I haven't.
LEO: Right. So ... (?)
MAGGIE: How's your mum?
LEO: Dead.
MAGGIE: Oh.
LEO: Couple of years back. No surprise. You know she loved her cakes.

MAGGIE: …
LEO: She liked you. Always asked after you. I don't think she ever understood. Why you—
MAGGIE: You shoulda told her.

Beat.

LEO: How are you?
MAGGIE: I'm sick.

Beat.

LEO: How bad is it? Do you—? I can organise a doctor or—
MAGGIE: No thanks.
LEO: I know a great surgeon.
MAGGIE: That's not why I—
LEO: He owes me.
MAGGIE: Everybody owes you!

Beat.

LEO: Still at the bank?
MAGGIE: Still running your own?
LEO: [*nodding*] You know me, I'm a regular Robin Hood. Helping the 'have-nots'.
MAGGIE: And then you terrorise them.
LEO: 'Course these days I'm more interested in red on the books than splashed on the walls. But try telling the kids. They all want to be gangsters, packing knives and guns and fucking nunchucks. Nunchucks? Christ! Your brother didn't need that shit. Props, he called 'em. These days there's no class. I blame the drugs.
MAGGIE: Stop selling them.
LEO: Not a social call then?
MAGGIE: Prosper Deng. You loaned him money.
LEO: Did I?
MAGGIE: How much?
LEO: What's it to you?
MAGGIE: I'm a friend.
LEO: Friend?
MAGGIE: … I meant—
LEO: With one of—
   Wow.

ACT THREE

That is
Wow.
MAGGIE: How much?
LEO: You tell your brother yet? Good thing he's a vegetable.
MAGGIE: [*turning to leave*] Fuck you!
LEO: When he came to me, your 'friend', he was already in deep. He owed money to hock shops, loan sharks, people all over town. I helped him roll it over.
MAGGIE: With you.
LEO: That's what I do.
MAGGIE: How much did he—?
LEO: Eight.
MAGGIE: They can pay you four now.
LEO: And the rest?
MAGGIE: …
LEO: [*laughing*] Oh, you must be sick.
MAGGIE: You won't even miss it.
LEO: Four thousand dollars?! Maggie, come on, I'm a reasonable man, but I've got three kids in private school. That doesn't cover a semester.
MAGGIE: These people, they've got nothing.
LEO: That's not true. They've got my money.

Beat. MAGGIE *takes out her cheque book.* LEO *laughs.*

MAGGIE: What?!
LEO: Nothing.
MAGGIE: …
LEO: It's just—is this the girl I knew growing up? So tight with a penny, so afraid to follow in her father's footsteps.
MAGGIE: I'll give you six and we're done.
LEO: Maggie, stop. You're embarrassing us both. Look, if you want a favour. Just ask.

MAGGIE *starts writing out a cheque.*

MAGGIE: Eight thousand.
LEO: Borrowed. But that doesn't account for the interest.
MAGGIE: How much?
LEO: Give us a tic.
Times thirty per cent.

Compounded weekly.
That's it!
Ooh.

MAGGIE: How much?

LEO: You don't want to know.

MAGGIE: Leo.

LEO: Eighty.

MAGGIE: Thousand?!

LEO: If he pays today.

MAGGIE: He's dead.

LEO: It's a curly one.

Beat.

MAGGIE: I don't have that much.

LEO: 'Course you don't. That's how this works.

MAGGIE: If I give you twenty. Today.

LEO: Maggie, why are you doing this? The son can pay it or let the mother. From what I've heard she's quite—

MAGGIE: YOU LEAVE HER ALONE!

LEO: …

MAGGIE: I can give you twenty now.

LEO: You can… But that'll barely make a dent. And meanwhile the remainder keeps ticking over.

MAGGIE: Let them go.

LEO: You know the game.

MAGGIE: Cancel the interest.

LEO: You want me to—okay…
But. If I do. That would be a favour.
Which I'm willing to do. But it does beg the question. What can you do for me?

Beat.

MAGGIE: I don't do that anymore.

LEO: Shame.

MAGGIE: …

LEO: You met the boy? Good kid. Loves his mum. I see a lot of potential.

MAGGIE: Stay away.

LEO: Come back to work for me.

MAGGIE: …
LEO: Either you do or they do.
MAGGIE: … I can't
LEO: I understand you don't want to. There's things I don't want to do, things I hate to do, but I will if I must.
MAGGIE: Like Col?
LEO: I tried to save him!
MAGGIE: You destroyed him!
LEO: Christ, I bent over backwards to keep him on the job—you think anyone else would touch him? The man was a drunk! He'd come in eight in the morning three sheets to the wind.
MAGGIE: AND WHY WAS THAT?!
Christ, Leo, the things you had him do.

> *Beat.*

LEO: I'm sorry, it's them or you.
MAGGIE: … I need time.
LEO: Sure. Take all the time you can afford.

> MAGGIE *gets up to go.*

When I was a kid, I used to think pawnshops were for chess—you could buy extra pawns there to replace the ones you lost. But the word comes from 'peon'. Peasant. They're just foot soldiers you send out first in pursuit of the queen. It doesn't cost, see, to lose them. They're worth fuck all.

SCENE TWO

The Deng house. Kitchen. AMATH *and* BENNY *are scrubbing the wall,* GEORGINA *supervising.*

MAGGIE: [*to* GEORGINA] What are you doing here?
GEORGINA: We've got it all sorted out now, Maggie, [*to* AMATH] haven't we?
MAGGIE: We have to go.
Now.
GEORGINA: It's lucky I came by.
MAGGIE: I told you—pack your things.
GEORGINA: There. See. It's coming out.

MAGGIE: Amath?
GEORGINA: I think with a little more Jif—
MAGGIE: Now!
GEORGINA: We're really starting to get somewhere.
BENNY: Mum?
MAGGIE: We have to go!
AMATH: Where?
MAGGIE: …
AMATH: This is our home. We will stay.

    AMATH *goes on scrubbing the wall.*

MAGGIE: This man your husband borrowed from. He won't stop.
AMATH: How do you know?
MAGGIE: It doesn't matter.
BENNY: Who is he?
GEORGINA: A little harder, Benny.
MAGGIE: You can't fix this with a working bee.
BENNY: Who?!
GEORGINA: Oh, for God's sake, leave them alone.
MAGGIE: Oh, you must love this.
BENNY: / Who is he?!
GEORGINA: What?
MAGGIE: Being back in the fold. Being there for her.
BENNY: TELL ME WHO HE IS!

    Beat.

MAGGIE: He runs a pawnshop in Bowden.
GEORGINA: Oh, for heaven's sake.
MAGGIE: It's a front. Trust me, you don't want to owe a man like Leo Hermes.

    Beat.

AMATH: I will talk to him. Explain how things are.
MAGGIE: That won't work.
BENNY: Ask for more time.
MAGGIE: This isn't Centrelink, he's a fucking shark!
GEORGINA: I am sure if she talks to him—
MAGGIE: NO! You can't negotiate with a man like Leo. People wind up hurt.

ACT THREE

BENNY: How do you know?
MAGGIE: I used to work for him.
GEORGINA: Oh, Maggie.

> AMATH *shoots her a look: 'How could you?'*

MAGGIE: [*to* AMATH] I did it for Col!
When he first went into hospital—Leo put him into private. He paid for a round-the-clock nurse, the works. Then, a few months later he starts twisting the screw. Asking me to make referrals. People we'd turned down for loans. People maybe he could help.
AMATH: Who?
MAGGIE: A woman. [*Beat.*] She wanted a loan to start up a business. But her credit rating, see...
I knew no other bank would touch her.
AMATH: And so you gave her to this man.

> *Beat.*

MAGGIE: [*nodding*] A couple of months later, she fell behind with her payments...
GEORGINA: I would have called the police.
MAGGIE: She did. Things escalated.
BENNY: What happened?
MAGGIE: Oh, grow up, what do you think?!

> *Beat.*

AMATH: How many others did you send to him? How many others did you—?
MAGGIE: None.
AMATH: I don't believe you.
MAGGIE: I never did it again. Not even when your husband—

> *Beat. They all stop.*

BENNY: What?
MAGGIE: We have to / go.
BENNY: What did you say?
MAGGIE: We don't have time for—
BENNY: You tell me what you said!

> *Beat.*

MAGGIE: ... He came to me for a loan. Prosper.

AMATH: No.
GEORGINA: Goodness.
AMATH: And you refused him.

Beat. MAGGIE *nods.*

BENNY: And now my dad is dead.
MAGGIE: Benny—
BENNY: Because of you.
MAGGIE: I never meant to—
AMATH: Why did you refuse him?
MAGGIE: …
AMATH: You could see he was in trouble. That without it he would suffer. You could have saved him. But you didn't. Why didn't you?
MAGGIE: I don't know.
AMATH: You do.
MAGGIE: I don't.
AMATH: Why?
MAGGIE: I already told you—
AMATH: Why?
MAGGIE: I swear to you I—
AMATH: Why?
MAGGIE: Because he was black, alright! Fuck him! [*Beat.*] Come see my brother. Come see what they did to him. Six of them. Six of you. He'd quit collecting, got himself a job at a nightclub in town. And then his first fucken night…
It wasn't personal. Col asked them to leave and then they …
What kind of animals—?
AMATH: Stop. My husband didn't cause your brother's accident. *You* did.
BENNY: Just like you killed my dad.
AMATH: Thank you for the warning. But this is family business. We will fix this ourselves. Get out.
GEORGINA: You heard her.
AMATH: Both of you.
GEORGINA: What?
AMATH: You're like hyenas tearing over scraps of my pain.
GEORGINA: Oh, I don't think that's true.

ACT THREE 49

AMATH: You don't want to help me. Either of you. You want to keep us dependent. Reliant. Useless.
GEORGINA: Now now. We only want the / best for you.
MAGGIE: You don't know who you're dealing with.
AMATH: No, it is you who don't know who you are dealing with! You treat us like children but we are stronger than you think. We are survivors.
MAGGIE: If you stay—
AMATH: I am tired of running.
MAGGIE: [*reaching out to her*] Let me—
BENNY: DON'T YOU TOUCH HER!

He shoves MAGGIE *hard against a wall.*

I wish you had never come into our lives.

BENNY *runs out of the house.* AMATH *starts after him.*

GEORGINA: [*to* AMATH] I'll go.

Beat. MAGGIE *catches her breath.* AMATH *picks up the sponge and continues to scrub.*

MAGGIE: Please… I want to help.
AMATH: [*laughing*] Of course. [*Beat.*] Do you know what is a mosquito net?
MAGGIE: A mosquito net?
AMATH: There was a woman in our camp. Rasheda. She made these nets to sell and we worked for her.
There were eight of us, all women, all working for Rasheda. And the money—it wasn't much, but we earned it ourselves and this gave us pride.
Then one day an announcement. Your country decided to help us in the fight against malaria. And had donated one hundred thousand nets.
No-one can compete with charity.
And a few years later all the nets are torn but now there is no Rasheda and no means to make more and so we are forced to cry to you for more aid. And you resent us for asking and we resent you for making us ask.
If only someone had asked us to begin with. 'What do you need?'

We could have told them.
But no-one ever asks.
MAGGIE: ... I can fix this.
AMATH: All these things you do for us...
You want forgiveness. You want me to love you. But you cannot love yourself.
I was wrong to trust you.
MAGGIE: No.
AMATH: You are a lizard. A snake with legs.

> AMATH *closes the door in* MAGGIE*'s face.*
>
> *Driveway.*
>
> MAGGIE *is alone. Beat.* GEORGINA *enters.*

GEORGINA: Little shit. And after all we've done.
Let me tell you—I'm a good person. I am. I give to UNICEF. I donate to Greenpeace, I buy dolphin-safe tuna and free-range eggs—even though they're more expensive. And pink ribbons for breast cancer, red ribbons for AIDS and the white one for—I forget what it's for but I always pin one on!
MAGGIE: I need thirty thousand dollars.
I've got the rest, but we still come up short.
GEORGINA: Thirty thousand?
MAGGIE: Thirty-two. That and eight from the bank plus forty of my own and Amath will be clear.
GEORGINA: ...
MAGGIE: Georgie?
GEORGINA: I see... And when do you need it?
MAGGIE: Today.
GEORGINA: Thirty thousand? Right.
MAGGIE: I know it's a lot but—
GEORGINA: And we'll get it back?
MAGGIE: No.

> GEORGINA *laughs nervously.*

This isn't something you can fix with a soup kitchen.
GEORGINA: I'm thinking. [*Beat.*] It's just—it's a lot of money.
MAGGIE: It is.

ACT THREE

GEORGINA: I think we should call the police.
MAGGIE: No.
GEORGINA: This is a matter for them.
MAGGIE: There's no proof. And if you go after Leo—
GEORGINA: I have a family.
MAGGIE: So does Amath.
GEORGINA: I know. But.
MAGGIE: Georgina?
GEORGINA: It's best we don't get involved. Don't you think?
MAGGIE: Best for who?

> *Beat.* GEORGINA *opens her purse, presses a note into* MAGGIE'*s hand.*

GEORGINA: Here.
MAGGIE: A hundred.
GEORGINA: Good luck.

> GEORGINA *exits.*

SCENE THREE

The pawn shop.

LEO *is sitting.* BENNY *standing.* LEO *nurses a baseball bat across his knees.*

LEO: Your dad's dropped you in the shitter, hasn't he?
BENNY: …
LEO: My old man. On my eighteenth birthday you know what he gave me? It was a ledger he kept of all the expenses it had cost him to raise me. There was even the fee charged by the doctor for delivering me. I used to think he was a prick. But he was trying to teach me something…
BENNY: Did you pay him?

> *Beat.* LEO *picks up the baseball bat, approaches.* BENNY, *frightened, holds his ground. Beat.* LEO *puts the bat in* BENNY'*s hands.*

LEO: I've got a job for you. And I think you're going to like it.

SCENE FOUR

Happy Time Mini-Mart.

MAHIRA *is behind the counter. The bell rings.*

BENNY *enters wearing a hoody, carrying the baseball bat.*

MAHIRA *looks up, sees* BENNY. *Looks to the exit.* BENNY *shakes his head.*

MAHIRA: Please.
BENNY: Open the till.
MAHIRA: You don't have to—

> BENNY *raises the bat, about to swing.*

Stop!

> MAHIRA *opens the till.*

You see.

> BENNY *tosses a Coles bag to her.*

BENNY: In the bag.

> BENNY *looks around, clearly nervous as* MAHIRA *fills the bag.*

MAHIRA: Tell me. Does it make you feel powerful? To rob a woman?
BENNY: …
MAHIRA: You are working for him. Aren't you?
BENNY: …
MAHIRA: [*swearing in Arabic*] You tell him I will not be intimidated. Do you hear me?!

> *She slides the bag back to him.*

Now go.
BENNY: And the safe.
MAHIRA: Please, that is everything.

> BENNY *slams the bat down on the counter.* MAHIRA *cowers, cries out.*

BENNY: Open it!

> *Beat.* MAHIRA *stops, staring at him.*

MAHIRA: … You are him… The boy from before.
BENNY: Give me the money!

ACT THREE

MAHIRA: Why are you doing this? You bring shame on your house.

> BENNY *is pacing the floor, trying to calm himself.* MAHIRA *reaches out.*

BENNY: GET BACK!

MAHIRA: This is not right!

BENNY: The safe!

MAHIRA: You want to kill me? Fine. I came here to build a life for my family. With honour. You are a liar and a thief! Just like your father.

> BENNY *hits her. Both are stunned. Beat.* MAHIRA *wipes the blood from her lip.*

BENNY: I'm sorry.

MAHIRA: You think I'm afraid of you.

BENNY: …

MAHIRA: You are nothing.

> BENNY *screams, swings the bat, then at the last moment turns away and starts smashing up the store. He overturns shelves and smashes produce, burning up all the rage inside him before finally collapsing in a heap.*

SCENE FIVE

The Deng house. Night. Late.

A knock at the door.

AMATH, *in a nightgown, answers.*

AMATH: Benny, is that you?

> AMATH *opens it. It's* LEO.

LEO: Hello, darlin'.

> *Beat.*

AMATH: Please. Come in.

END OF ACT THREE

ACT FOUR: RED

SCENE ONE

Minimart. MAHIRA *is behind the counter.* BENNY *is still in a heap on the floor. He is weeping.*

The bell. MAGGIE *enters.*

A look between MAHIRA *and* MAGGIE. *She points* BENNY *out. She nods. Beat.*

MAGGIE: Benny?
BENNY: Why don't you leave us alone?
MAGGIE: I'm proud of you.
BENNY: [*laughing*] Hasn't Mum told you? She thinks I don't know but I do. Who I am. *What* I am.
MAGGIE: You're her son.
BENNY: I tried to fit in. I tried to be Aussie but I am not. I am African. A rape baby. Born from hate. Just like the men who bashed your brother. That's all I'm good at.

    Beat.

MAGGIE: They didn't start it.
BENNY: What?
MAGGIE: It was Col. He was drunk. He gets. When he's had a few.
…
On the CCTV. It was him. Not them. Him. Understand? Not them. Not you. [*Beat.*] Your mum loves you so much.
BENNY: But she never asked for me.
MAGGIE: No.
You were a gift.

SCENE TWO

The Deng house. Night. Late. The lights are off.

The phone rings continuously. The radio is on. Talkback about unwanted troublemaker Sudanese refos in Adelaide.

ACT FOUR

MAGGIE *and* BENNY *enter. Chairs upended. Signs of struggle.*

BENNY: Mum?
MAGGIE: Amath?!
BENNY: Mum, are you here?
MAGGIE: Amath, it's us.
BENNY: Where is she? What if something—?

> *Sobbing. Soft. Coming from the kitchen.*

Mum? Where are you?
MAGGIE: Shhh.

> *Beat. They listen.* MAGGIE *opens the cupboard under the sink.*
>
> AMATH *is huddled there, terrified.*

BENNY: Mum!

> BENNY *rushes to her. Tries to pull her out. She resists.*

MAGGIE: She's in shock.
BENNY: Mum, what happened?

> LEO*'s alarm goes off.* AMATH *shrieks.*

It's okay. Shhh. I'm here.

> MAGGIE *ignites a lighter, a small circle of light. She surveys the room. A body in the corner.*

MAGGIE: Shit.
BENNY: What is it?
MAGGIE: Look after your mum.

> MAGGIE *approaches the body. Kneels down. Holds up the lighter to it.* LEO *lies slumped in the corner, a smear of blood down the wall. Amath's kitchen knife is in his stomach.*

Oh, Christ.
BENNY: What?
MAGGIE: Look away.
BENNY: Shit! Mum? What did you do?

> AMATH *starts to babble in Dinka.*

Mum?
MAGGIE: What is she saying?

BENNY: I don't know.
 … Something about a Kenyan.

   Beat. AMATH *continues rambling.*

MAGGIE: She's in shock. Get her out of here.
BENNY: Where?
MAGGIE: The bedroom. Keep her warm. Then you call the police. GO!

   BENNY *helps* AMATH *to her feet, then out of the room. Beat.*

   MAGGIE *approaches* LEO. *She kneels to retrieve the phone.*

LEO: Mags.

   MAGGIE *startles.* LEO *goes into a coughing fit.*

Fuck, who'd have thought she had it in her?

   Looking down at the knife, he coughs.

Crazy bitch.
MAGGIE: Leo…
LEO: I'm sorry, Mags.
MAGGIE: …
LEO: I won't stop. They owe me now. Blood will have blood.
MAGGIE: Leo, please?
LEO: You know it, love. I'll see them burn for this.

   MAGGIE *picks up the cushion beside him. He sees her. She hesitates.*

Remember those sunsets down at the port. You, me and Col, feet dangling off the jetty. Sipping beers and shucking oysters from the bag. It was perfect.
MAGGIE: I remember.
LEO: You know I fancied you.
MAGGIE: … I know.
LEO: Before I knew you—before I knew you weren't interested.
MAGGIE: Let them go.
LEO: I can't.
MAGGIE: For me.
LEO: You know me, Mags.
 People don't change.
MAGGIE: They can.

ACT FOUR 57

LEO: Not the big things.

> *Beat.*

MAGGIE: I never thanked you. For coming to see Col. You didn't have to do that.

LEO: I did.

> *Beat.* MAGGIE *nods. She holds the cushion over his face. He struggles. It's violent. She holds grimly on. Finally he goes still.*

SCENE THREE

Two concurrent scenes: MAGGIE *at the hospital;* AMATH *at the bank three years later. Throughout this split scene the light slowly dims.*

        MAGGIE: Heya, Col.

AMATH: Deng.

        MAGGIE: How ya been?

AMATH: Amath Deng.

        MAGGIE: Nice room.

AMATH: Yes, of course.

        AMATH *pulls out paperwork from her handbag.*

        MAGGIE: Who'd you fuck?

AMATH: Sorry?

        MAGGIE: But you need—

AMATH: A carer.

        MAGGIE: A shave.

AMATH: Part-time.

        MAGGIE: [*holding her nose*] Time for a bath too.

AMATH: But I'm studying to be a nurse.

        MAGGIE: Listen, I gotta tell you something.

AMATH: My son Benedict.

        MAGGIE: The thing is—

AMATH: An apprentice mechanic.

        MAGGIE: I won't be coming in for a while.

AMATH: And my daughter Grace.

        MAGGIE: It's advanced.

AMATH: In a few weeks.

MAGGIE: I'll be dead.
AMATH: She'll be four.
MAGGIE: You know, 'high cost of living'.
AMATH: A home loan.
MAGGIE: Yeah.
AMATH: I have savings.
MAGGIE: It's my heart.
AMATH: And also this reference from a friend.
MAGGIE: Life's a bitch and then—
AMATH: She died.
MAGGIE: Doc said too little too late.
AMATH: Thank you.
MAGGIE: I just hope—
AMATH: I am ready.
MAGGIE: When they weigh the scale—
AMATH: I want to do this on my own.
MAGGIE: You know the balance?
AMATH: No, no other debts.
MAGGIE: I guess that's why I'm here.
AMATH: We are 'in the black'.
MAGGIE: To say I'm sorry.
AMATH: What is the saying?
MAGGIE: And I forgive you.
AMATH: 'The future is bright.'
MAGGIE: And—
AMATH & MAGGIE: Thank you.

THE END

www.ingramcontent.com/pod-product-compliance
Lightning Source LLC
Chambersburg PA
CBHW050023090426
42734CB00021B/3390